Sleeping In

Kyle C. Miller

BookLeaf Publishing

Presentation by *BookLeaf Publishing*

Web: www.bookleafpub.com

E-mail: info@bookleafpub.com

ISBN: 9789357440295

First edition 2023

DEDICATION

Dedicated to all my heroes, whose standards I should have held higher.

Late at Night

Wide awake here in my bed,
I thought of all the things that could have been.
The girl in class who smiled at me when I was set on living free.
That summer job that came and went and all the money that I spent.
Forgotten friends who I dearly miss,
replaced with nights of loneliness.
All the time my brain can find,
remind me of when I was unkind.
Late at night, my thoughts are deep
I wonder why I cannot sleep.

I see you

I see you there with those fake eyes
hiding under that disguise
to shield the diamond in the rough
the men can search but won't find much.
It shelters you from rain and wind
but it's now time to shed your skin.
Alone and cold out in this storm
come take my heart to keep you warm.

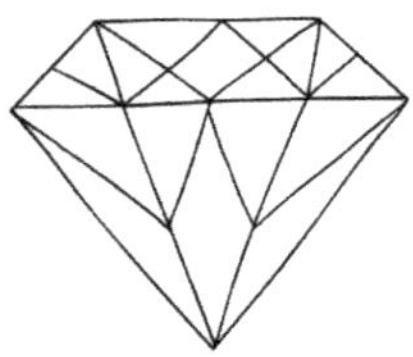

Loaded

Let's get loaded together
on life
on love
and in the morning
we can sweat it out
arm-in-arm dancing
the can-can
with the sun
shining upon us
Let's get loaded together
in the night
off cheap wine
and dark chocolate
laughing
as the moon arrives
and wraps us up
together
in her black blanket

Legends Never Die

Bukowski came to me in my dreams,
Speaking of heroes, laughing at legends
Drunk on wine with bottles at his feet
Warning about the whiskey and women
and fires of the soul
Fires so hot
it burns
man
alive
Women and whiskey and fires of the soul
There is nothing for them
But words

Someplace New

I feel like I just want to leave here
And go someplace else
Until I get tired of being alone there too
And that's how I'll live my life
Running from place to place
Where I can fall asleep in peace
And dream of somewhere new.

Pink Walls

The screams echo
in the halls
of Bach and Beethoven.
Van Gogh and Munch,
drape the walls
and
Dali is etched in concrete.
We read Thompson,
Hemingway
and
take our pills like,
Kerouac.
There is no escape
I am caged
In white shackles
against white walls
But
I don't see white walls.
I see pink walls
and blue couches
green beds
yellow toilets
I brush my teeth at red sinks,
look into mirrors that are black.
There is no white in my world.

The house with a heart

I am within and without
I am the moonlight on the bookshelf behind you, sitting next to the fire, reading.
I am both cracked walls and vintage paintings above you as you turn the page.
I am the air that fails to take your breath away.
I am a dirty carpet and creaky floorboards.
I am the Victorian chair covered by your blanket.
I am an old room, quiet and lonesome.
You are here, making yourself comfortable.

Lock it in

Sweat it out
Pour it out of you
Drain it from the typewriter
Flow it from the microphone
Explode from your workouts
Sweat out the thoughts, the ideas, the stigmas
That they have given you
Shit it out
Cry it out
Laugh it out
Lose your mind in the process
Find out what remains
Lock it in
Block it off
Wrap a police ribbon around it,
warn others not to come near
Protect the tiny pieces of who you are
and set fire to the rest

Searching for perfection

At night when we drink ourselves to pieces
we hope to put ourselves back together again,
In hopes of becoming a better person.
Hangovers remind us that we were destroyed
and rebuilt in a single night.
But we haven't figured it out yet.
So, we begin again.

Pitter - Patter

My head goes pitter-patter pitter-patter
When everyone else goes tick-tock.
In this regular world, I'm regularly irregular
bearing a heart beating
Ba-Dum Ba-Dum instead of Lub Dub Lub Dub
Sometimes I wish it would stop
while everyone else keeps on going
Until then
My typewriter goes
Click
Click
Click
While theirs says nothing at all

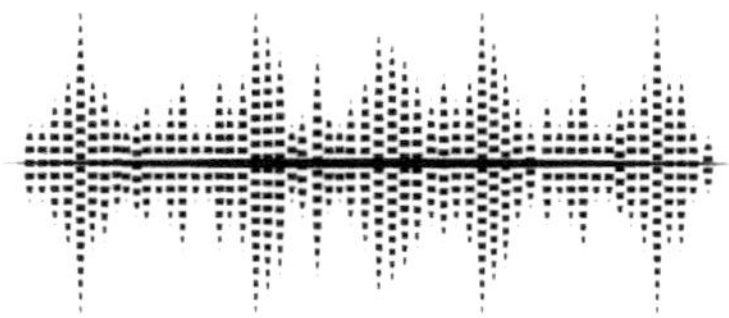

Best Wishes

I hope you choke on the lies you say to him
Words that were meant for me
Standing on the altar with lights too dim
I send you best wishes too
for a long honeymoon headache
that lasts until you both are through
I hope it lasts forever
The pain of your mistake
I'll find somebody better
someone who isn't fake

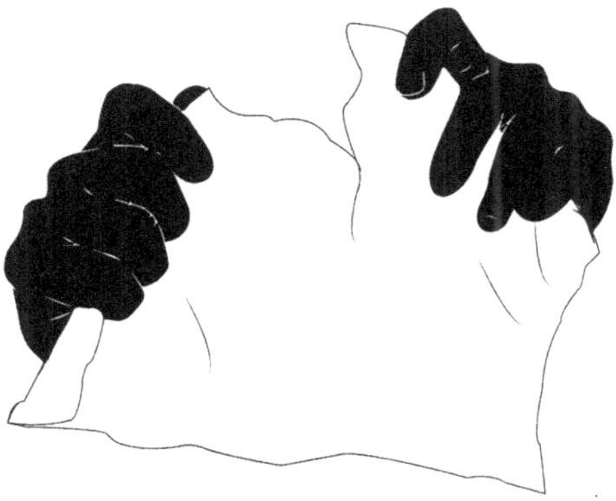

Beauty in everything

There is beauty in the things that take effort
and it is there when it falls apart.
There is beauty in laughter, and it stays for the
tears.
There is beauty in women and among men,
and there is beauty in love between them.
The sky is beautiful and so is the rain
when the clouds come to let the sun take its rest.
There is beauty all around us
and when we look and can't find it,
there is beauty in that too.

Change your shirt

Self-harm isn't always just razor blades on forearms
or overeating or drinking yourself to sleep.
Sometimes, it's going to bed without brushing your teeth
or driving without a seat belt on.
It's going days without a shower
and wearing the same shirt every day for comfort.
It can be watching tv endlessly without eating
and drinking enough caffeine to make you ill.
It shows in the way you sit in your car for hours staring out the windshield
while making empty promises.
Like the ones, you made to us,
about getting help.

Hummingbird Heart

If you want to love me and
don't know where to start,
come take a listen to my hummingbird heart.
Give him water,
sing him a song
Hear him softly,
start to sing along.
Look at him asleep in his little cage.
He grows a bit tired every day.
Take him out.
Set him free.
Watch him fly away
in the summer breeze.

Ugly paintings full of hope

Pictures hang on the wall, and we see the torn canvas and broken frames
Until a friend comes along, takes a picture, and shows us its beauty.
We take a second look and know that they are right and deep down we hope they see us that way too.

Religion

Religion doesn't find me behind church pews
It hears my 911 calls from abandoned buildings and
broken-down cars late at night
when it's too tired to pick up the phone.
I leave messages and, in the morning, it calls to tell me to
come home.
But I already have a home,
with a warm bed,
that I am constantly running from.

Angels and Demons

Did you forget that angels can descend from heaven too
burning as hot as demons do?
Who said they weren't harmless?
That their smiles cannot easily show fangs
that their handshake wouldn't turn into a closed fist...
directed straight at you?

The Parade of Women

Here come the ponytails,
the hair buns,
the straight hair,
the hair in their face
their hair on my face
the braided hair
and the corn rows.
Each with a set of eyes,
those damn eyes
blue eyes
green eyes
blue and green eyes.
With flashes
lashes
some with slow dashes.
All looking at me,
coming for me,
attacking me,
all while smiling.
big lips
small lips
red lips
come here and kiss me lips
Begging me to stay
but I run away
hidden behind closed doors
writing about those damn eyes.

When we let down our Angels

He was two days dead.
I wrote a letter to my angel
asking if she was ok.
It's still raining up in heaven
And they haven't let the shades up all-day
Blaming themselves for people
They could have helped but were too late
The rest of us grieve.
Throwing rocks at their windows,
wishing to see their heavenly faces.
Hoping that one day
they won't give up on us
as easily as we do,
on ourselves.

Brown Paper Bag

My heart can beat like this
It can beat like that
It beats over here
over there.
Often,
I don't think it beats at all.
It is best described by other people
in their own words,
I wish,
I could have said first.
But, it is my heart and not theirs.
I carry it in a brown paper bag down the street.
Sometimes, late at night,
I give it to other people when it is hungry,
but I never let it get too full.

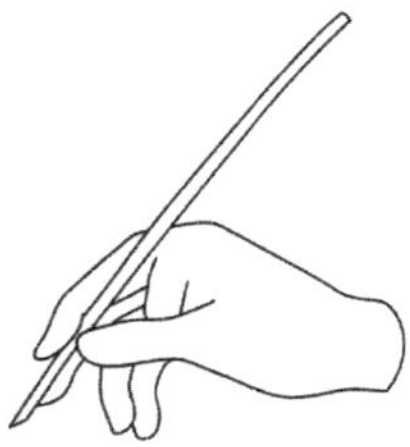

Sleeping In

The day has the sun, and the night has the moon.
The happy people dance and the lonely poet drinks.
At dawn, we all wake up and wait for the peace that dusk brings.

www.ingramcontent.com/pod-product-compliance
Lightning Source LLC
Chambersburg PA
CBHW062111140826
49812CB00058B/1298
* 9 7 8 9 3 5 7 4 4 0 2 9 5 *